FunTime® Piano

Rock 'n Roll

2010 Edition

Level 3A–3B

Easy Piano

This book belongs to: ______________________________

Arranged by

Nancy and Randall Faber

Production Coordinator: Jon Ophoff
Design and Illustration: Terpstra Design, San Francisco
Engraving: Dovetree Productions, Inc.

FABER
PIANO ADVENTURES®
3042 Creek Drive
Ann Arbor, Michigan 48108

A NOTE TO TEACHERS

FunTime® Piano Rock 'n Roll is a collection of hits from the rock and roll era that is sure to entertain the piano student. The selections have been carefully arranged for the early-intermediate pianist. A variety of keys are used, including major and minor, and the tempos range from upbeat rock to slow ballad.

This material offers the student music which is fun to play and, at the same time, helps develop a strong rhythmic sense.

FunTime® Rock 'n Roll is part of the *FunTime® Piano* series arranged by Faber & Faber. "FunTime" designates Level 3 of the *PreTime® to BigTime® Supplementary Library*, and it is available in a variety of styles: Christmas, Classics, Favorites, Hymns, Jazz & Blues, Popular, More Popular, Ragtime & Marches, and Rock 'n Roll.

Following are the levels of the supplementary library, which lead from *PreTime® to BigTime®*.

PreTime® Piano	(Primer Level)
PlayTime® Piano	(Level 1)
ShowTime® Piano	(Level 2A)
ChordTime® Piano	(Level 2B)
FunTime® Piano	(Level 3A–3B)
BigTime® Piano	(Level 4)

Each level offers books in a variety of styles, making it possible for the teacher to offer stimulating material for every student. For a complimentary detailed listing, e-mail faber@pianoadventures.com or write us at the address below.

Visit **www.PianoAdventures.com**.

Helpful Hints:

1. Since rhythm is of prime importance, encourage the student to feel the rhythm in his/her body when playing popular music. This can be accomplished with the tapping of the toe or heel, and with clapping exercises.
2. Hands-alone practice is often helpful. Ensure that the playing is rhythmic, even when playing hands separately.
3. The songs can be assigned in any order. Selection is usually best made by the student, according to interest and enthusiasm.

About Rock 'n Roll

The beat of rock 'n roll captured the spirit of the youth and the attention of the music industry in the 50s. With its upbeat rhythm, rock 'n roll proved irresistible to all young people.

Pioneers such as Chuck Berry, Fats Domino, and Little Richard led the way for the rock 'n roll king—Elvis Presley. Other greats such as Bill Haley, Carl Perkins, and the legendary Jerry Lee Lewis made significant contributions to the new music form. Bolstered by the rise of celebrity disc jockeys and Dick Clark's "American Bandstand" on television, the sound spread quickly throughout the U.S. and soon to Britain. There it was picked up by The Beatles and The Rolling Stones who, in the 60s, went on to usher in yet another rock era.

ISBN 978-1-61677-023-5

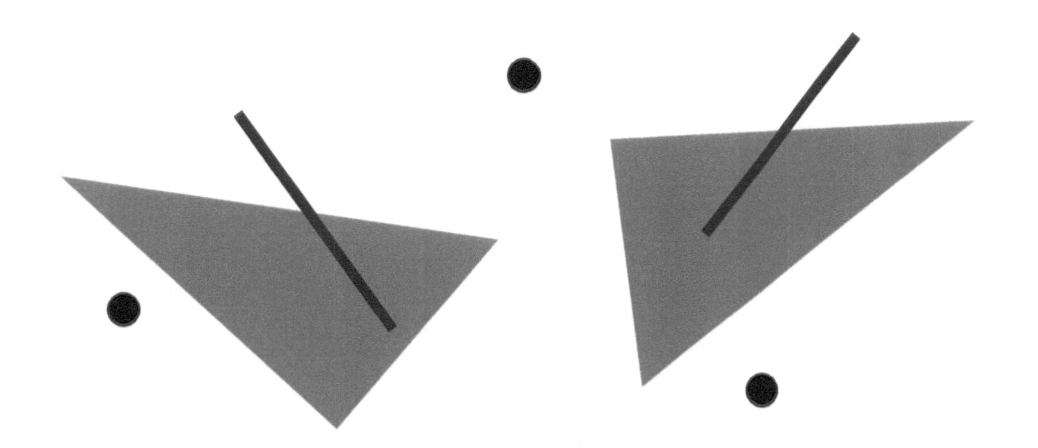

TABLE OF CONTENTS

All I Have to Do Is Dream

BOUDLEAUX BRYANT

12
taste your lips of wine, an - y time, night or day.
15
On - ly trou - ble is, gee whiz, I'm dream - in' my life a -
18
way. I need you so, I could die. I
mp
21
love you so, and that is why when - ev - er I want you
24
all I have to do is dream.
rit.

Rockin' Robin

13
go, Rock-in' Rob-in, we're real-ly gon-na rock to - night.
16
Fine
Pret - ty lit - tle ra - ven at the
mp
18
bird band - stand taught him how to do the bop and
20
it was grand. Start - ed go - in' stead - y, and
22
D.S. al Fine
bless my soul, he out - bopped the buz-zard and the ori - ole.
f

Bye Bye, Love

FELICE BRYANT and BOUDLEAUX BRYANT
Moderately fast
There goes my ba - by___ with some - one
mf
4
new. She sure looks hap - py;___
7
I sure am blue. She was my
10
ba - by___ till he stepped in.
mf

13
Good - bye to ro - mance that might have
16
been.
Bye bye,
f Bye bye,
19
love.
love.
Bye bye, hap - pi - ness.
Bye bye, sweet ca - ress.
22
Hel - lo lone - li - ness, I think I'm gon - na
Hel - lo emp - ti - ness, I feel like I could
25
1.
cry.
2.
die. Bye bye, my love, good bye.
rit.
mp

Come Go With Me

Words and Music by
C.E. QUICK

17
f
Yes, I need you, yes, I real-ly need you. Say you'll nev - er
20
leave me. Say, you nev - er, yes, you real-ly nev - er,
23
nev-er give me a chance. Come, come, come, come,
mf
26
come in-to my heart. Tell me, dar - lin', we will nev-er part. I
29
need you dar - lin', so come go with me.
rit.

Hound Dog

Words and Music by
JERRY LEIBER and MIKE STOLLER

13
8va
mf
They said you was high - classed,
but that was just a
16
lie.
They said you was high - classed,
19
but that was just a lie.
Well, you ain't
22
f
nev - er caught a rabbit and you ain't no friend of mine.
25
8va

Stand by Me

Words and Music by JERRY LEIBER, MIKE STOLLER, and BEN E. KING

night has come and the land is
dark and the moon is the on - ly light we
see, oh, I won't be a -
fraid, no I won't be a - fraid just as

21
long as you stand, stand by me. So
24
dar - ling, dar - ling, stand by me.
f
27
Stand by me. Oh, stand,
30
stand by me. Stand by me. Dar-ling,

33
stand
by
me.
Stand
by
f
36
me.
Oh,
stand,
stand by
me.
39
Stand by
me.
Stand by
me.
dim.
41
Stand by
me.
mp
8va
p
rit.
pp
8va

Howl at the Moon

NANCY and RANDALL FABER

17
f
21
mp
f
24
28
mf
dim.
32
mp
f
R.H.
rit.
8va

Hey Jude

Words and Music by
JOHN LENNON and PAUL McCARTNEY

15
1.
2.
- ter. Hey - ter.
19
mf And an - y time you feel the pain, hey Jude,
22
re - frain, don't car - ry the world up - on
26
your shoul - ders. And well, you

30
know that it's a fool who plays it cool
33
by mak - ing his world a lit -
36
- tle cold - er.
Na, na, na,
39
na, na
f
na, na, na, na.
p
mp
Hey
D.S. 𝄋 al Coda

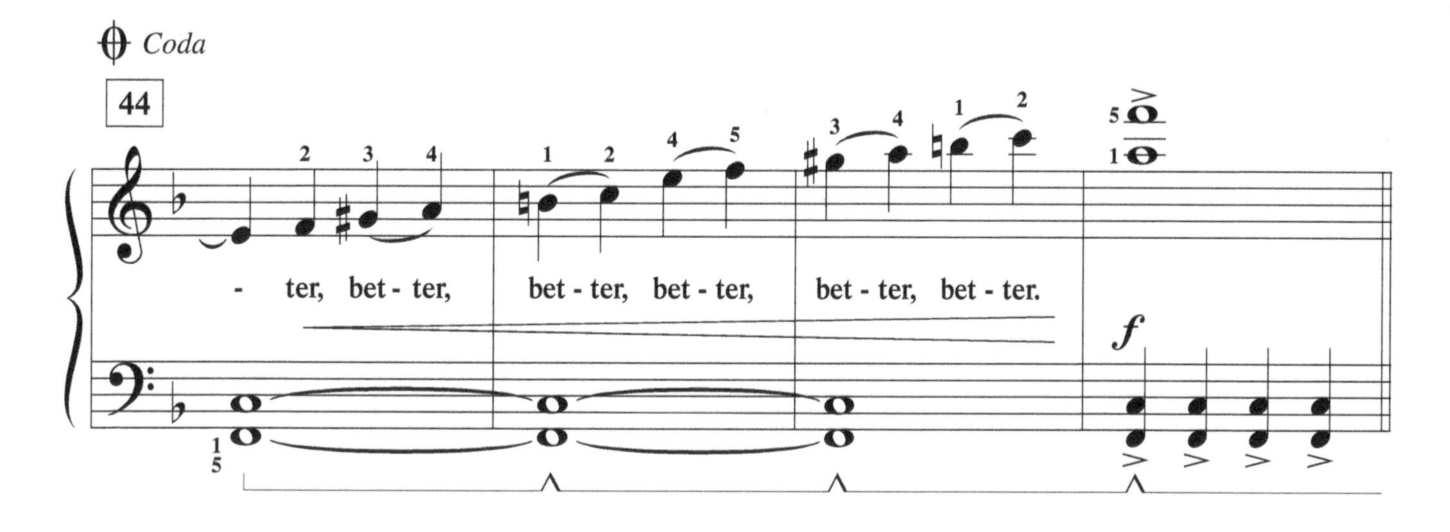
Coda
44
- ter, bet - ter,
bet - ter, bet - ter,
bet - ter, bet - ter.
f

48
f Na,
na,
na,
na, na, na,
na,

51
na, na, na,
na,
hey

54
Repeat ad lib.
Jude.
last time rit.
8va

Rockin' Pneumonia and the Boogie Woogie Flu

Words and Music by
HUEY P. SMITH

11
lov - in', ba - by, that ain't all.
I want to
13
kiss her but she's way too tall.
15
Young man's rhythm got a hold on me too,
I got the
17
rock - in' pneu - mo - nia and the boo - gie woo - gie flu.
f
20
8va
ff

Mumbo Jumbo

NANCY FABER

Mum - bo Jum -
bo!
Mum - bo Jum - bo!
Mum - bo Jum - bo!
rit.
8va

Runaround Sue

Words and Music by
DION DI MUCCI and ERNEST MARESCA

11
this girl will leave me with a
bro - ken heart.
Now, lis - ten peo - ple what I'm
14
tell - ing you,
a - keep a - way from
Run - around Sue.
17
Hayp, hayp,
bum - da ha - dy, ha - dy,
hayp, hayp,
20
bum - da ha - dy, ha - dy,
hayp, hayp,
bum - da ha - dy, ha - dy,
8va
23
hayp.
(8va)

The Last Night of Summer

NANCY and RANDALL FABER

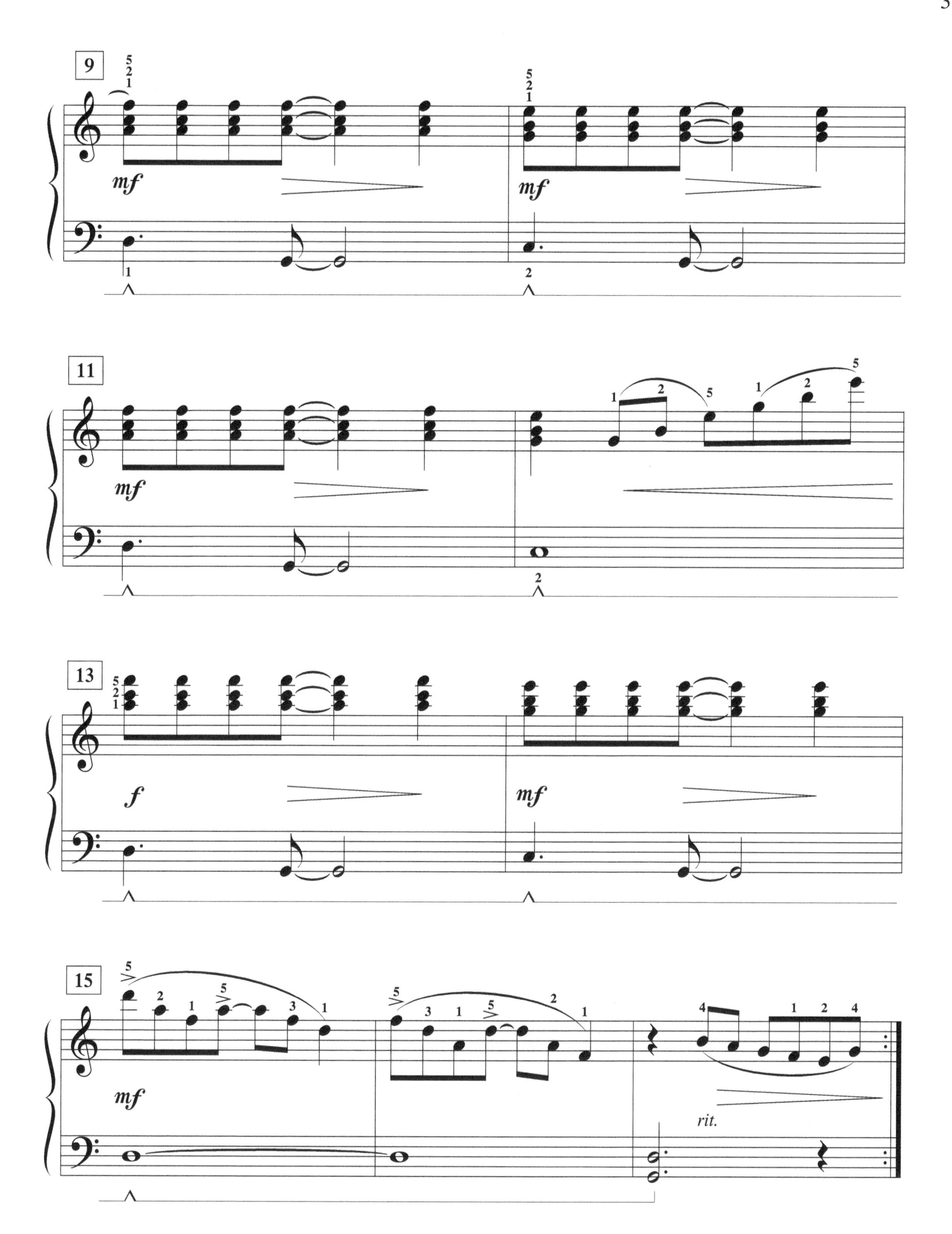
9
mf
mf
11
mf
13
f
mf
15
mf
rit.

18
Freely
mp
pp
20
mf
22
24
rit.
p
8va